Ways to Level Up your Mindset

Change your mind to change your world.

Margaret Robinson

Table of content

Introduction

Your mindset affects your success and happiness. You become what you think about.
The way we think shapes how we perceive the world. Your perception of yourself and others will be warped if yours is. Even if we are unaware of it, the way we think and feel influences how we act.
Success in life depends on having the correct mindset. Here's how you can improve yours. The significance of attitude
A frame of mind is a mindset. It is the culmination of all of the ideas we have about the outside world and ourselves. It serves as our lens of observation for the outside world.
Our opinions and thoughts are shaped by our education, religion, family, and experiences. Our intention is "set." It immediately affects how we perceive the world and behave. Like Amit The mind is a malleable mirror; change it to see a better reality, advised
While mindsets can shift, it takes time. While attitudes only have a momentary effect. They are simpler to alter because of this. Our mindsets are ingrained in our beliefs, so changing them takes extra work.
Your interpretations and reactions are predetermined by your attitude. Your relationship with the outside world and yourself are shaped by it. Pick your mentality carefully.
Your attitude can work for you or against you.
The most widely accepted theory on mindsets distinguishes between two categories: fixed and growth mindsets. the author of Mindset: The New Psychology of Success According to Carol Dweck, our capacity for learning is determined by our perceptions of our own intelligence. A fixed mindset is the conviction that our characteristics are unchangeable

permanent attributes. This way of thinking assumes that success is the sole result of talent. On the other side, a growth mindset holds that our intelligence can develop over time and via experience. This way of thinking motivates us to work harder because we know that effort yields better results.

While a fixed perspective restricts our ability to learn, a growth mindset enables us to realize our greatest potential.

But there are a lot more different kinds of attitudes. How we view the world impacts how we process emotions. A bad attitude might intensify our bad emotions. and keep us from moving forward.

Our thoughts have two consequences on us: They either constrain or free our potential.

For instance, binary thinking restricts our consideration to just two options. We perceive things via a right or wrong lens and think in terms of "one thing" or "the other."

Your frame of mind can enhance clarity or distort perception.

Chapter One

Improving mindset

I really believe that mentality is the key to both success and happiness. Everything in your life—from your thoughts and feelings to the way you act and respond to the outside world—is influenced by your mindset and set of beliefs. Your thinking must align with your desires if you want to succeed; otherwise, it can be keeping you from where you want to be.
Here are seven practical methods to improve your mindset:
Modify your inner dialogue
You can tell a lot about your mindset by the dialogues you conduct with yourself. Your thoughts will manifest into reality, and your attitude will prevent you from living the life you want, if you are telling yourself "I am not good enough to realize my dreams."you desire. Change your negative self-talk to an empowering speech to improve your mindset. Saying to oneself, "I can do this" or "I got this," may sound cliche, but it actually works.
- [ ] Alter the Language
Change the way you talk to other people after altering your inner conversation and the tale you are telling yourself. To promote a growth mentality, stay away from sayings like "I am always like this" or "I am always doing this." Additionally, develop the habit of focusing on the positive aspects of your life rather than whining and discussing your issues. This will

promote an attitude of abundance rather than one of scarcity and dread.

- [ ] Choose the mindset you require and behave accordingly. Pick a desired outcome. to do and think, "Which attitude do I need to accomplish this goal?" and "What kind of mindset do those who achieved this aim have?"

For instance, those who are physically fit and healthy may have the attitude that "I adore taking care of my body, nourishing it with natural foods and exercising every day."
Act as though you already HAVE the mindset of a healthy and active person if that is your objective. By doing things this way, you are essentially coaxing your brain into developing a new thought and supporting it with behavior.

Chapter Two

How to change your outlook to achieve success

Recognize your thoughts more clearly

Recognize that you need to change the way you think. Start by becoming more conscious of your thinking. Which lens are you employing to view reality when you respond to a situation or before making a decision?

Do you have a perfectionism mentality? Or a me-me-me one (and believe that everything in the world depends on you)?

- [ ] Refrain from viewing reality as a binary.

Most mental models are deceptive. They compel us to have a binary perspective on the world. Binary thinking produces a fictitious conundrum. When there are truly more possibilities, we behave as though there are only two.

Put your binary thinking to the test. Avoid the propensity to categorize everything as either-or, black or white, or right or bad.

- [ ] Consider your beliefs

Our beliefs are firmly rooted in our mindsets. Examining our belief system is the first step in changing our thinking.

What is preventing you? Do your beliefs empower you or impose restrictions on you? Determine which beliefs are beneficial, and attempt to change the unhelpful ones.

- [ ] Restate your life's purpose

Everyone desires to be a part of something greater than themselves. What do you want out of life? Find your purpose.
Make up your own criteria for success. What ways of thinking will bring you there? Choose the lenses that will enable you to fulfill your higher life's purpose.
The goal of discovering your life's meaning is not important. The trip is everything.
- [ ] Transform constrictive beliefs into empowering ones
Challenge your current perspectives. Revisit the analysis On point 1, you did.
What mentalities do you have that don't work for you? Although it is difficult, it is worth the effort to alter your perspective. Your filter must be changed in order to upgrade them.
Your thinking serves as the lens through which you view the world and yourself. Transform your limiting beliefs into freeing ones to improve your mentality.

"I failed to finish the assignment because I.." or "I'm running behind schedule today because..."
When anything went wrong previously, did you put the blame on the environment and move past the incident? Or did you use the chance to reflect on how you could have done things more effectively?
Both mediocre and successful people frequently encounter challenges. The approach is where there is a slight difference. While typical individuals blame the situation for their failures, successful people change themselves to overcome these challenging conditions.
You are avoiding some truths about yourself when you criticize and point the finger at others. So quit hiding your

mistakes and start taking responsibility. If not, it will be impossible for you to develop a successful mindset.

- [ ] Avoid errors rather than seeking out original ideas.

When I tried starting enterprises and trying to come up with a product that will revolutionize the market. I didn't realize how inadequate our sales and marketing abilities were.

You might think that in order to advance in your career, you need amazing ideas. You miss the small errors you make when looking for such ideas.

Establish a process for self-reflection to help you avoid both major and minor errors. Making sure you don't make mistakes won't instantly make you famous or rich. But as time passes, your results add up to a completely astonishing result.

It is amazing how much longer-term benefit people like us have received from striving to continuously not be stupid rather than attempting to be very smart intelligent

Chapter Three

Disequilibrium

Disequilibrium occurs when internal and/or external causes stop the market from reaching equilibrium or lead the market to go out of balance. This may be an immediate side effect of a shift in variable elements or the outcome of lingering structural imbalances.
A country's balance of payments deficit or surplus is referred to as being in disequilibrium.

KEY LESSONS

Disequilibrium occurs when a market's supply and demand equilibrium is disturbed by outside causes. As a result, the market transitions into a situation in which supply and demand are out of balance.
Disequilibrium can be brought on by a number of factors, including government intervention, labor market inefficiencies, and unilateral supplier or distributor activity.
Disequilibrium is typically eliminated when the market enters a new equilibrium state
As an illustration, individuals are motivated to begin creating more excessively priced things, boosting supply to meet demand and bringing the price back to balance.
Examples range from immediate incidents, such as flash crashes, to long-term occurrences, such as recessions and depressions.

When the amount provided and the quantity demanded in a market are equal at an equilibrium price or a market-clearing price, the market is said to be running efficiently. There are neither surpluses nor shortages of an item or service in an equilibrium market. Thus, market equilibrium is the condition in which supply and demand are equal and stable prices result.

In general, a surplus of goods or services leads to lower prices, which increases demand, whereas a shortfall or undersupply raises prices, which decreases demand. A state of equilibrium is produced by the influence of supply and demand balancing one another. When this adjustment of supply, demand, and/or prices does not function as predicted, disequilibrium results. Disequilibrium states frequently return to equilibrium as a result of market forces. This is so that investors will buy underpriced assets and sell ones that are overpriced for a profit, encouraging arbitrageurs to bring supply and demand back into balance.
Uncertainty in Action
Here is a fictitious graph showing the supply and demand for wheat. The price at Pe, as depicted in the graph, is the sole price that encourages farmers (or suppliers) and consumers to conduct an exchange. The supply and demand of wheat are balanced at Pe.

According to our graph for the wheat market, if prices rose to P2, providers would be eager to offer additional wheat to the market from their storage barns because the higher price would cover their production expenses and result in higher profits. However, given the higher market price for wheat, customers might buy less of it overall. When this imbalance arises, there will be a surplus since there will be more supply than demand, which will result in an unbalanced market.

The difference between Q2 and Q1, where Q2 is the quantity given and Q1 is the quantity demanded, in the graph serves as a representation of the surplus. Given the extra supply of the good, providers will want to sell the wheat as soon as possible before it spoils. According to our graph for the wheat market, if prices rose to P2, providers would be eager to offer additional wheat to the market from their storage barns because the higher price would cover their production expenses and result in higher profits. However, given the higher market price for wheat, customers might buy less of it overall. When this imbalance arises, there will be a surplus since there will be more supply than demand, which will result in an unbalanced market.

The difference between Q2 and Q1, where Q2 is the quantity given and Q1 is the quantity demanded, in the graph serves as a representation of the surplus. Given the extra supply of the good, providers will want to sell the wheat as soon as possible before it spoils. According to our graph for the wheat market, if prices rose to P2, providers would be eager to offer additional wheat to the market from their storage barns because the higher price would cover their production expenses and result in higher profits. However, given the higher market price for wheat, customers might buy less of it overall. When this imbalance arises, there will be a surplus since there will be more supply than demand, which will result in an unbalanced market.

The difference between Q2 and Q1, where Q2 is the quantity given and Q1 is the quantity demanded, in the graph serves as a representation of the surplus. Given the extra supply of the good, providers will want to sell the wheat as soon as possible before it spoils. and will continue to lower the purchase price. According to economic theory, if a free market is allowed to operate without any intervention, the price of wheat will eventually drop to Pe.

What if the wheat market price was P1? Customers are prepared to buy more wheat (Q2) at this price due to the decreased cost. Conversely, when the price is below the equilibrium price, suppliers will provide less wheat (Q1) for sale because they fear that it will be too cheap to recoup their marginal costs of production. Wheat will be in short supply when Pe reaches P1 in this scenario because there is a greater demand than supply for the good.

due to resources The market is said to be in disequilibrium when resources are not distributed effectively. In a free market, it is anticipated that as a result of the good's scarcity, the price will rise until it reaches the equilibrium price.

Disequilibrium Causes

Market disequilibrium can be attributed to a variety of factors. When a supplier establishes a fixed price for a good or service for a specific amount of time, disequilibrium occasionally results. If the market's demand for the commodity or service grows during this period of sticky prices, there will be a scarcity of supply.

Government action is another cause of unrest. The market may become inefficient if the government establishes a floor or ceiling for an item or service. The amount delivered is greater than the amount asked. For instance, if the government sets a cap on rent, landlords could be hesitant to rent out their spare properties to tenants, which would result in an excess demand for housing due to a lack of rental housing.

The labor market may experience disequilibrium from an economic perspective. When the government establishes a minimum wage—a price floor on the amount that an enterprise can offer its employees—it may cause a disequilibrium in the labor market. There will be an excess supply of labor in the economy if the required price floor is higher than the price at which labor equilibrium exists.

A country's balance of payments (BOP) is considered to be out of equilibrium when its current account is in deficit or excess. The balance of payments of a nation is a record of all business done with other nations over a specific period of time. The BOP's Current Account part contains information about the country's imports and exports of goods. a serious deficit On the current account, there would be an imbalance if imports were higher than exports.

There are large current account deficits in the US, UK, and Canada. A similar disequilibrium exists when exports exceed imports and a current account surplus results. Current account surpluses are particularly substantial in China, Germany, and Japan.

An imbalance between domestic savings and domestic investments can lead to a balance of payments disequilibrium. If domestic investments exceed domestic savings, a deficit in the current account balance will result because the extra investments will be financed with capital from foreign sources. Additionally, a balance of payments disequilibrium will emerge when the trade agreement between two countries influences the volume of import or export operations.

Additionally, modifications to an exchange Disequilibrium can result from a country's currency being revalued or depreciated. Inflation or deflation, fluctuations in foreign exchange reserves, population expansion, and political unrest are further reasons that could cause an unbalanced situation.

Chapter Four

Persuasion

How persuadable must your workers be? People in the workplace typically fall on a spectrum. Some people find it extremely difficult to persuade others to take action, while others seem to have the ability to sell water to a well. Of fact, the majority of us lie in the middle of these two extremes.

You can strengthen your workplace relationships, manage more skillfully, and make wiser hiring decisions by being aware of the persuasive personality feature.

What does the term "persuasive" mean?

A person with persuasive personality features can influence others to act, think, or purchase items. How they go about it differs greatly and frequently is determined by their general personality type (A, B, C, and D in our tests).

Some persuasive individuals possess powerful, self-assured personas that Others frequently follow suit. Others might be affable and charismatic, while still others might be extremely intelligent rationalizers who present the evidence to support their position, and so on.

What matters is that persuasive people are more successful than average at persuading others to support their cause, regardless of how they go about it.

What characteristics define a compelling person?
Here are a few indicators that someone has a propensity for persuasion:

They attract others with their charismatic personality and enthuse them.
They confidently express their thoughts and opinions.
They take the necessary steps to make their argument and, in general, aren't scared to bring up issues that others might be hesitant to bring up.
They frequently prosper in situations especially those in client-facing or promotional positions like sales, public relations, law, and other professions, but they may be found in all kinds of careers.
working with someone who is compelling

Making use of your persuasive employees' strengths enables them to use their persuasiveness for the benefit of the entire team.

How to become more persuasive
Give background. Giving them as much background knowledge as you can will help them have a better understanding of the big picture since you can be sure that your persuasive staff will soon start introducing fresh concepts and methods of operation.
Even if they are not in leadership positions, persuasive personalities are frequently born leaders. Train your

persuasive team to execute things correctly, and you might discover The remaining team members comply.

How to encourage a persuasive person

Honor their accomplishments. Sometimes managers rely too much on their persuasive staff without taking the time to consider how their abilities help the team as a whole. This is particularly true for "soft talents" and interpersonal relationships, which can offer significant, concrete advantages.

Your persuasive staff shouldn't be subjected to pointless rules and norms for interpersonal communication. Let them operate normally so that they can use their gift. The consumer is plainly getting more irritated as the cashier steadfastly repeats the complete corporately mandated series of upsells, cross-sells, and rewards program material (under fear of firing). Give your workers more authority when they demonstrate that they can be relied upon to use good judgment. freedom to choose their own strategy.

How to critique someone who is compelling

Sometimes, whether intentionally or unconsciously, persons who are extremely persuasive can take charge of a meeting. Make sure you're setting the agenda and communicating all the topics you need to when you need to provide feedback. Listen to them out if they want to offer input. But make sure to state the core idea once again. Send a follow-up email summarizing the main points.

What does being persuading not mean?

Like some people are born persuasive, some lack the ability to persuade others to agree with them. What does the term "unpersuasive" mean?

People who lack persuasiveness find it more difficult to persuade others to agree with their opinions and thoughts.

There are numerous reasons why someone could come across as unpersuasive, just like with a persuasive person. However, in the end, the unpersuasive employee finds it more difficult than usual to persuade others.

In addition, some persons succeed at persuasion in particular settings (such as a small group discussion with people they know well) but find it difficult in others (such as presenting in front of larger groups).

What characteristics define someone who is not persuasive? Some warning indications that a person isn't usually persuasive are:

When they have to persuade someone else to do something, purchase something, or believe anything, they don't feel at ease.
They could be when their persuasiveness is on the line, they become anxious.
They would rather let someone else do the convincing.
How to influence someone who is not persuadable

People who lack persuasiveness don't naturally promote themselves or their ideas as much as those who do. Retaining outstanding talent can be greatly aided by learning to pay a little bit more attention.

How to train a resistant worker
Indicate to the employee when to speak up. Let them know to loop you in as quickly as possible, for instance, if they aren't getting the reports they require from other departments in a timely manner.

You might wish to provide ongoing coaching on how to be more persuasive and aggressive depending on the role. Most people require training and experience to develop confidence. public speakers and presenters.

How to inspire a non-persuasive person

Make sure you are considering their requirements at work. Do they struggle to get around obstacles? Is there anything from another department that they could use? Find out how you can speak up for them. Don't wait for them to express their aspirations, ambitions, or preferred working conditions. Some people find it difficult to express their needs and wants. Give them time to reflect throughout your one-on-one conversations while also allowing time for queries to be answered. Be accessible in a variety of ways (in person, via email, and via business chat) so that the employee can utilize the communication method that suits them the most.

How to provide constructive criticism to a skeptic employee

If the employee's effectiveness at work is being hampered by their inability to persuade, offer advice on how they might do better. Persuasion is a skill that can be learnt, but persuasiveness is a personality feature.

Find out what works for your staff by working with them. Do they need to take notes before a meeting to make sure they have all they need to say? Do they fare better with phone calls or emails as follow-ups? Not everyone must employ the same techniques.

Give after-the-fact feedback to an employee who is working on speaking up in group situations. Speaking up can be much easier for more reserved types if they receive positive reward when they do so.

Chapter Five

Social change Effect

Human interactions and relationships have a profound effect on society by transforming cultural and social institutions over time. This process is known as social change. Many of us either don't fully grasp or take social change for granted. Any society that has existed has changed over time. Every day, something changes. Change is something we all accept as inevitable, so it must be the end of the story. Not quite, I suppose.

Social change, according to sociologists, is the transformation of social and cultural institutions as a result of changes in interpersonal connections and interactions. These alterations take place gradually and frequently have substantial effects on society that last for a very long time. Social movements for women's rights, civil rights, and LBGTQ rights, to name just a few, have all contributed to well-known examples of this type of transformation. Institutions, relationships, and cultural norms have all changed. These social change campaigns have affected conventions. That is some really complex information. Don't you think so?

Our ability to affect societal change as a group intrigues me, and I hope it intrigues you as well. While we acknowledge that change is inevitable, we do not have to accept that it leaves us unable to combat it. The degree to which we care about the course of social development determines our ability to try to influence it and contribute to the kind of "change we hope to see in the world." It doesn't matter if Gandhi actually said these things. What important is that the expression raises the query, "What type of change do we hope to see in the world?"

I ponder this topic every day as the executive director of the Global Citizens Circle (GCC), a nonprofit organization with a history of more than 43 years, as I seek to further the organization's objective to promote positive change in our local communities, our country, and our planet. Since Southern New Hampshire University (SNHU), our partner and host institution, aspires to "change the lives of students," I imagine that SNHU also considers this subject frequently. As it works "to improve the effectiveness of action for progressive social change," our Belfast-based partner, The Social Change Initiative (SCI), undoubtedly gives it some thought. All three of us care about social change and are aware of our power to affect it positively. Different strategies may be used by us to affect change. GCC achieves this through debate among participants with various viewpoints and backgrounds. SNHU accomplishes this by providing accessible and cutting-edge social science degree programs online, along with related campus majors and, as of late, even in refugee camps in Africa. SCI wields its impact through bringing together donors and social activists from all around the world.

These are undoubtedly big objectives that require our undivided attention and limitless creativity in order to imagine a better future. That's fantastic, but you might be wondering why you should care, why you should take time out of your extremely busy schedule to do something, and, more importantly, how you might even start contributing to constructive social change. I want to say that if we start now, it's not that difficult. the most fundamental level, that of developing relationships.

The first step in change is how and when we interact with others.

We take the first step in listening when we show respect to those whose opinions and life experiences differ from our own. We also acknowledge that there are numerous perspectives and points of view on the majority of pressing issues. We must engage in dialogues that push and tug and require us to give and take if we are sincere about wanting to be a part of meaningful change. And if we're prepared to do that, we can identify those areas of agreement and unite around them. We don't have to give up the ideas that make up our core beliefs; instead, we should discover methods to cooperate in order to bring about change that represents our shared beliefs. It is the ability to make more significant changes through the art of principled compromise.

For more than 40 years, the Global Citizens Circle has brought various groups of people together for thought-provoking discussions on a variety of topics, including economic equality, conflict resolution, and reconciliation. Protestants and Catholics from Northern Ireland have sat down together and talked about their shared desire for peace. We've entertained South African exiles who were previously branded "terrorists" in their own nation before rising to prominence there. We have sat influential businesspeople beside the homeless and disenfranchised, activists alongside professors, and we have witnessed the change that has taken place at our discussion circles.

Chapter Six

City Epistemology

Street epistemology is a movement that uses philosophical techniques in casual talks to persuade individuals to adopt beliefs in trustworthy ways. Professional philosophers may write books and papers, but anyone who appreciates the truth can respectfully discuss how views are known to be true with friends, family, neighbors, and other members of the community.

The intention is to motivate both ourselves and others to consider the criteria we employ to assess the veracity of truth claims in order to enhance the validity of our epistemology. While this may lead to people coming to different conclusions, it is not the intended outcome. The crux of the debate, according to Dr. Boghossian, "is not altering beliefs, but changing the way people create beliefs." Neither party should be concerned about so long as a high bar for justification is set, one can be led to adopt a false view. It is entirely up to the individual to make use of the realization that they may have reached a belief using an unreliable approach. They are never forced to hold a particular opinion or to take actions that are not in their best interests.

The foundation of street epistemology is the combination of socratic methods and the study of epistemology. Socratic techniques encourage an interlocutor—your discussion partner—to respond to thoughtful inquiries. In most circumstances, asking the right questions will help you find unreliable justifications. The more you comprehend epistemology, however, the easier it will be for you to recognize when an interlocutor's implicit epistemology may be suspect and the more credible alternatives you will be able to provide. Additionally, you'll be more prepared to converse with others whose claims explicitly draw on apologetics or other epistemological theories.

The philosophical concepts employed in Street Epistemology will next be discussed in more detail. Consider reading an introductory philosophy book or enrolling in an online course if you have never delved into epistemology. watching the epistemology videos from Crash Course Philosophy and Wireless Philosophy.

Reliabilism, or the idea that what justifies one in maintaining a belief is the truth-conduciveness of the process by which one arrived at the belief, is the concept that best captures the epistemology upon which Street Epistemology is built.

It matters how you get at your beliefs since it has an impact on your likelihood of holding correct beliefs. Our stated objective of reducing reliance on flawed epistemology implies reliability. Because we are fallible as a species (we cannot "know that we know"), we settle for procedures that, even in the face of scant proof, allow us to have a reasonable amount of faith in the veracity of statements.

The Street Epistemologist, however, is not Dogmatic: We will utilize any theory of epistemology and any form of justification as a tool, provided that it tends to support true claims rather than false claims with an appropriate level of confidence for the type of claims at hand. We employ both inductive and deductive reasoning, just like everyone else, while keeping an eye out for fallacies. Being human, we also learn a lot of our beliefs through testimony (while also being aware of its flaws, and we are unable to avoid making intuitive coherentist assessments of the plausibility of new assertions. However, falsifiability—the justification method that drives most of modern science—is what we emphasize with Defeasibility Tests. Additionally, we employ Bayesian inference to compare and assess the likelihoods of conflicting hypotheses and apply Occam's razor to favor the most straightforward process that might produce the observed phenomena

. By continuing the chain of justification until it reaches ordinary claims and determining whether the inference is valid, we'll even delve into the justification of extraordinary claims in a fairly foundationalist approach. When applying Outsider Tests, Street Epistemologists are being pragmatic, as we look for the real-world outcomes that allow us to decide between conflicting claim.

Chapter Seven

The Street

Every time a truth assertion is made, Street Epistemology can be applied. However, it serves unusual claims—such as those involving miracles and other supernatural occurrences—the best.

existence of one or more deities or other spiritual beings (theism).

Natural law violations or suspensions of natural law (supernaturalism, paranormal and psychic phenomena, miracles, karma).

One's existence as a conscious being does not stop with biological death (afterlife, reincarnation, resurrection).

The success of healing techniques that conventional science-based medicine dismisses as worthless or lacking in proof (quackery).

An idea or system's scientific legitimacy if it has never undergone sufficient inquiry, fails scientific testing, or both (pseudosciences).

Certain events or circumstances are the result of a powerful yet hidden force or group, and there is evidence to support this is absent (conspiracy theories).

The Street Epistemologist questions whether the following arguments are strong enough to support confidence in the claim in these circumstances, where we frequently encounter them.

Description

Don't Push It: Persuade Instead! You must know a lot of people who need to change, yet despite your best intentions, they continue to fight because change generally causes people to feel uneasy. Margaret Robinson is not only a salesperson but also a father, friend, and consultant. He outlines a straightforward, repeatable, predictable, and moral approach that will allow you to guide people in discovering for yourself what and why they need to change, drawing on his extremely successful sales history and decades of research.

Robinson's sensible counsel, which is illustrated by a variety of occasionally humorous, occasionally touching, and always instructive stories, will help you make sure that changing someone's mind is never an act of compulsion but rather a positive experience for them one of compassion and care.

www.ingramcontent.com/pod-product-compliance
Lightning Source LLC
LaVergne TN
LVHW020539160826
845677LV00015B/4142

* 9 7 9 8 3 5 4 3 8 6 1 1 6 *